# Uninvited
# Guests

# Uninvited Guests

POEMS

## Donald Glazer

GREEN WRITERS PRESS | *Brattleboro, Vermont*

Printed in the United States

10 9 8 7 6 5 4 3 2 1

Green Writers Press is a Vermont-based publisher whose mission
is to spread a message of hope and renewal through the words and
images we publish. Throughout we will adhere to our commitment to
preserving and protecting the natural resources of the earth. To that
end, a percentage of our proceeds will be donated to environmental
activist groups. Green Writers Press gratefully acknowledges support
from individual donors, friends, and readers to help support the
environment and our publishing initiative.

*Giving Voice to Writers & Artists Who Will Make the World a Better Place*

Green Writers Press | Brattleboro, Vermont
www.greenwriterspress.com

ISBN: 979-8-9883820-6-5

INTERIOR ILLUSTRATIONS:
AeRhee Lee and Ellis Paul

PRINTED ON 30% POST-CONSUMER FIBER WITH STOCK SHEETS THAT ARE FOREST
STEWARDSHIP COUNCIL® (FSC®) CERTIFIED THAT COME FROM MANAGED FORESTS
THAT GUARANTEE RESPONSIBLE ENVIRONMENTAL, SOCIAL, AND ECONOMIC PRACTICES.
PRINTED BY PURITAN PRESS, HOLLIS, NEW HAMPSHIRE.

*With gratitude to those*
*who inspired these poems*

# Contents

I

II

### III

*Visitors*

Poems seldom knock
Unannounced
They barge right in
Uninvited guests

## Tenth Reunion

Raucous

We ran butterflies off the roof

Not knowing where the race would end

Nor when

A decade apart

We part again

*Winter*

When    Whim    Wove

Winsome patterns

Hours forever

*For Michael and Elizabeth's Wedding*

Headwaters join in Boston
Fed by the melting snow
Wide and deep
A channel grows

Where once two streams
One now flows
Fed by love
A river runs
Beneath the Houston sun

—·—II—·—

*The Proposal*

You say no
An early Spring
Left rosebuds
Stillborn
In the falling snow

## Mirrors – Twentieth Reunion

From across the room
You catch my eye
Your smile bridges twenty years

Then later
Lying here
Side by side
Two old friends
Giggling
At reflections of what might have been

## Midnight

Sounding through the walls
Bounding to the tambor's call
Lovers sigh
In drumbeats of delight
Down dark hallways
Out of sight
Passion punctuates the night

## Second Anniversary

Number two
How's the view
A slew of images recur
A blur of visages renew
Imaginary
Déjà vu
Imagine

## Katrina II

Six words are all it takes
You sound just like your Mom
And the levee breaks

## Family Therapy

Tell all, he says
We do
Ringing true
Like wind chimes
In a storm
Tuneful
While breaking up

*First Blood*

Your tongue
Stiletto sharp
Finds its mark
You always know
Just where to cut

*Parting Ways I*

Like peeling stamps
Damp or dry
No matter how we try
The corners tear

*Double Overtime*

Bittersweet, you say
Last night you saw the Celtics play
And stuck it out
Despite the heat
Uncomplaining all the way

Bittersweet for you not me
For me there's just the irony
That as you cheered
I lay in bed alone
Listening to the play by play

A year apart now
Day to day
We go our separate ways
Still in my heart I wish I knew
Why you could never play my way
And why, while we were two
The focus always had to be on you

## Spring

Spring slipped by so softly
It almost seemed as if
We were last in love
Not ten years past
But last
But last

*Brambles*

At first I barely noticed
The garden was so lush
And I was flush in our beginning

Then later, through the flowers
I could better see the thorns
And spreading weeds
But the roses
The roses blinded me

Until one day
Bushes overgrown
Entangled in the brush
The brambles blocked my way

*Parting Ways  II*

Snow swirling
Dense as fog
You drive off
Still smouldering
A half-burned log

*Trying Again*

Like an old shoe
Comfortable
For a while
But still causing blisters

You drive off
Though out of sight
Your spirit glistens
As I listen to the night

Seduced by you
Still soothed by you
I cradle my guitar
And softly sing your name
Caressing the refrain

*You*

It's not the view
But where we are
And what you bring
That makes me sing

*Balancing the Books*

You have too much red ink
Your chief comptroller says
Better write her off

*Taps*

I meant to write a barefoot poem
Skipping lightly above the grass
No thorns to trip its feet
Nor trees with apples to entice
I meant to fill a jug of verse
With lines from paradise

A summer song
Wine and beer
A summer frolic
Sophmore year

But heed the fears of former years
Don't place your faith in nymphs and dreams
Don't trust too much in fairy beings
They're not real
But bring real tears

The apples on the tree were ripe

Take a bite I say

To stay the taps that Autumn plays

You shake your head

No way, you say

The sun is gone

Our day is done

You turn your back

And walk away

## Desire

Old friends rushing down the hall
A chance encounter
Warm hello
You brush my thigh
Sparks fly

Attracted to the fire
I dreamt of you last night
*Tyger, Tyger, burning bright*
Eyes ablaze
Burning with desire
Desire is the fire

*Forbidden Fruit*

Just once
Just a taste
Not the whole tree
Tasty or not
Curiosity killed the cat
Not me

Tasty but not exactly new
Like apple pie and ice cream
Another helping please?

## Dreams

You come in
I close the door
In the silence plays
A now familiar melody
Gold and gray

Through your dress I press your breast
You touch my thigh
I close my eyes
And for a moment drift away

A sudden knock
You straighten up
Come in, I say
You say it's wrong
That's how it seems
But can't there be
A little place
In busy lives
For dreams?

# Muck

## I
*(Reality)*

You get angry
Start to yell
And dredging up the past
You pour
A bucketful of smelly muck
Around the floor

I try to tiptoe out the door
But slip and fall
And get caught up


## II
*(Wishful Thinking)*

You get angry
Start to yell
And I say
"Go to Hell"

*Hard Rain*

The wind shifts
Storm clouds appear
Your words like hail
Sting
As the cold front nears

*November*

Seasons run
Like you
I knew
The time had come
Maybe not forever
But for now

Behind gray walls
Our private garden bloomed
Beneath a shaded sun
Roped in
It was all we could allow
Maybe not forever
But for now

*Breaking Up*

Observations done
You set your microscope aside
And rinse the slide

## Megan's Bay

The hot spell snapped last night
No more balmy days
Overcast the paper says
I say gray

Good friends we've had
Good friends we've lost
Bob Marley plays
*Love's still burnin' through the night*
*Everything's gonna be alright*
Just stay away from Megan's Bay
No woman
No cry

But blue skies beckon far away
What's right seems wrong
What's wrong seems right
Donny heads for Nanny Cay

*Tans*

Looking back
Love faded with the waning sun
Winter comes
As we
Once one
Wonder what has gone

*Alone on Sunday Morning*

Teasing out the truth
Not what
But why
Not that you left
But why you didn't try

## Dawn

Dreams die a sudden death
A flash of light
A siren sounding in the night
Daybreak seeping through the shade

Still half-asleep
He wakes to see
A spot of blood turned gray
On sheets worn bare
Where they once played
And last night
In a dream
His lover
Still
She lay

Dreams die a sudden death
But only slowly fade away

## Dusk – On Learning of Nancy's Death

The crescent moon
Rips scythe-like through the night
Ravishing the waning light
Slashing stars

## Davy Blumberg

Davy's dead

Not yet ten

God gives and takes

Don't ask why

The rabbi says

יִתְגַּדַּל וְיִתְקַדַּשׁ שְׁמֵהּ רַבָּא

*Magnified and sanctified is the name of the Lord*


But facts don't lie

*Absalom, Absalom*

My son, my son

King David cries

The child dies

While bloody eyes

Hide

Behind the gray December sky

*Meyer Goldstein, 1900–1977*


The choir chants *Adon Olam*
A heldentenor anchoring the rest
East transplanted West

The Cleveland Indians lost today
Bums you laugh
Still echoing off walls you built to last

Never young to me
Always bald
For me you never aged
Even now
Gut long gone
A tree about to fall
Why we ask
Prometheus 'til the last

*Nightfall: For Ethel Glazer, 1921-2011*

Ready as you think you are
The time is never right
When dusk fades to night

## Biding Time

Lurking just around the corner

Skulking in the grass

Marking time

As seasons run

Waiting

Knowing that its time will come

*Nachum and Treini d. 1941*

The temple burns
The torah fuels the flames
Trapped inside
You struggle to escape the fire
The bema is your funeral pyre

On the wall at the top of the stairs
I see you every day
Looking out from a plain black frame
Side by side
Gazed fixed
Blind to a day still years away
A small town near Warsaw
I still hear my mother (your granddaughter) say

In my brother I see Nachum's nose and eyes
Neil Terry, named for both of you
In my daughter Mollie, Treini too

Besides these photos and your names

The only record that remains

Of your lives

These likenesses of you still survive

Embers

From the rubble and the flames

*Tracks*


High above
A hawk surveys the field below
Small tracks
New-fallen snow